Leading Lady

TIPPER GORE

Written by Julie Bach

Published by Abdo & Daughters, 4940 Viking Drive Suite 622, Edina, Minnesota 55435.

Library bound edition distributed by Rockbottom Books, Pentagon Tower, P.O. Box 36036, Minneapolis, Minnesota 55435.

Copyright ©1993 by Abdo Consulting Group, Inc., Pentagon Tower, P.O. Box 36036, Minneapolis, Minnesota 55435. International copyrights reserved in all countries. No part of this book may be reproduced without written permission from the copyright holder. Printed in the U.S.A.

Photos Credits: Bettmann pgs. 17, 24, 29
Black Star pgs. cover, 5, 8, 10, 14, 23
Archives pgs. 12,13

Edited by Rosemary Wallner

LIBRARY OF CONGRESS CATALOGING-IN-PUBLICATION DATA
Bach, Julie S., 1963-
 Tipper Gore / written by Julie Bach.
  p. cm. — (Leading Ladies)
 Includes bibliographical references (p.) and index.
Summary: Presents the life of Tipper Gore focusing on her childhood, education, work with the music industry, and involvement in her husband's political career.
 ISBN 1-56239-220-4
 1. Gore, Tipper, 1948- -- Juvenile literature. 2. Gore, Albert, 1948- -- Juvenile literature. 3. Vice-Presidents' wives -- United States -- Biography -- Juvenile literature. [1. Gore, Tipper, 1948- . 2. Vice-Presidents' wives.] I. Title. II. Series.
E840.8G66B33   1993   973.929'092--dc20   93-15326

TABLE OF CONTENTS

Thinking About Tomorrow 4

A Lonely Childhood 6

Falling in Love 7

Life in the Sixties 9

The Tug of Politics 15

A Campaign for Clean Music 16

Running for President 20

The Accident 21

The 1992 Campaign 22

A Strong Friendship 25

The Importance of Family 26

A New Role in Politics 28

Glossary 30

References 31

Index 32

THINKING ABOUT TOMORROW

On a warm night in July 1992, the Democrats were gathered for their national convention in New York City. Inside the enormous convention hall, thousands of people were cheering. They had just nominated Bill Clinton and Al Gore to run for president and vice-president of the United States.

On the brightly lit podium, two women embraced each other. They danced a lively boogie. They looked almost like sisters—same haircut, same style of clothes. Who were these women, and why were they so happy?

The women were Tipper Gore and Hillary Clinton. In November 1992, their husbands would be elected the youngest vice-president and president of the United States. Together the four of them would break many barriers. They were part of a new generation in politics.

Six months later, in January 1993, Tipper Gore stood beside her husband on the steps of the nation's Capitol Building. She watched him take the oath of office.

Tipper Gore (L) and Hillary Clinton embrace during the nomination of their husbands at the Democratic National Convention.

How had she come to this prestigous position? What kind of a vice-presidential wife would she be?

A LONELY CHILDHOOD

Tipper Gore was born Mary Elizabeth Aitcheson in 1949. Her mother, Margaret Odom, gave her the nickname "Tipper" from a favorite children's lullaby.

Tipper's father was John Aitcheson. Her parents' marriage did not go well. A few years after Tipper was born, the couple divorced. "The marriage was a mistake except for Tipper," her mother once said.

Tipper was sensitive about her parents' divorce. She remembers children teasing her for "having no father." She saw her father every Sunday, but that wasn't the same as having him at home.

After the divorce, Tipper and her mother moved in with Tipper's grandparents in Arlington, Virginia. The house was big and beautiful, but Tipper was lonely there. She had no sisters or brothers. Her mother worked many hard jobs to make ends meet. Her grandmother watched soap operas all day.

No one gave Tipper encouragement to try new things or be successful. "I was raised not to do anything except get married and have children," she says.

FALLING IN LOVE

In 1965, Tipper met Albert Gore, Jr., at a high school dance. He was a handsome and serious young man. Tipper was immediately attracted to him. And he was attracted to her. He called her the day after the dance. He wasn't very good at making small talk on the phone, but Tipper liked him anyway.

Shortly afterward, Al invited Tipper to his parents' farm in Carthage, Tennessee. Tipper must not have known very much about farm life. She came downstairs for breakfast the first morning with her hair done up and makeup on. But that wasn't enough to end the romance.

Al Gore came from a famous family. His father, Albert Gore, Sr., was a U.S. senator. His mother, Pauline Gore, was one of the first women to graduate from Vanderbilt Law School.

The Gore family house in Carthage, Tennessee.

Al had grown up in a political family, and he felt pressure to be involved in politics, too.

Al had spent half his childhood on his parents' farm in Carthage, Tennessee. He had spent the other half in Washington, D.C. His sister, Nancy, was ten years older.

Tipper knew about Al's political background. She looked at him as "a man who is going to make my life very interesting." And she knew she wanted to marry him. Soon after they met they began talking about how many children they wanted to have.

LIFE IN THE SIXTIES

After graduating from high school in 1966, Tipper went to the University of Boston. Al went to nearby Harvard University. They went to college in the late 1960s, a time of great change in the country. The civil rights movement was in full swing. Many people were using drugs. And protests against the Vietnam War were growing. Tipper and Al were caught up in the excitement of these times. They both believed strongly in equality for all people. They were both against the war.

Vice-President Al Gore's father, Tennessee Democratic Senator Albert Gore, Sr.

Tipper and Al looked forward to graduating from college and spending a happy life together. Then, in the summer of 1969, the Vietnam War interrupted their plans. Al was ordered to register for the draft. If his number was picked, he would have to go to war.

Al had protested the war because he felt the United States should not be fighting in Vietnam. He did not want to go. But his father's senate seat was up for reelection. Al knew that if he dodged the draft, as so many young men were doing, his father would lose the election.

It was a difficult decision. How could he fight in a war he believed was wrong? But how could he let his father down?

Finally, partly to help his father and partly out of his own convictions, Al registered. He was sent to Vietnam in 1970, just after he and Tipper were married.

Al never forgot the suffering and horror he saw in Vietnam. He was disgusted with the United States' role in the war. By the time he returned, he was disgusted with U.S. politics altogether. And his father had lost the election anyway.

The U.S. Army fighting in Vietnam in 1970. Al Gore was sent to Vietnam just after his marriage to Tipper.

In the 1960s the civil rights movement was in full-swing. Shown above is a demonstration led by the Rev. Dr. Martin Luther King, Jr.

Tipper, with her family on the campaign trail, from left: Kristin, Karenna, Sara and Albert Jr.

THE TUG OF POLITICS

Al and Tipper moved to the country near Carthage to live a simple life. They wanted to be away from politics. Al worked as a reporter at the *Nashville Tennessean*. Tipper worked as a photojournalist. For the first six years of their marriage, they didn't talk about politics. But it was always in the back of their minds.

Then, in 1976, Al suddenly decided to run for U.S. Congress. Tipper had always known that her husband probably would be a politician. Still, it wasn't easy to give up her new career to help him campaign.

To her surprise, Tipper found that she was a good campaigner, even though she was pregnant with their second child. Their first child, Karenna, had been born in 1972. Al won the election. Suddenly, Tipper was a politician's wife.

Her life now was split between Washington, D.C., and Arlington, Virginia. In Arlington, she and Al bought the house she had lived in as a girl.

In 1983, Al ran for a seat in the U.S. Senate. He won the election, but his victory was marred by grief. His older sister Nancy, who had always helped him in his political career, died of lung cancer in 1984.

A CAMPAIGN FOR CLEAN MUSIC

By 1982, Tipper and Al had four children: Karenna, Kristin, Sarah, and Albert III. Tipper worked hard at being a good mother. Her devotion to family eventually landed her in the fight of her life.

In December 1984, Tipper bought a record album for her daughter Karenna. When they listened to the album, they were shocked and angered by the violent lyrics about sex.

Tipper had grown up liking rock and roll. She listened to the Beatles, Rolling Stones, and Grateful Dead. She had even played the drums in an all-girl band. As a mother, she began to listen to new rock albums, especially from heavy metal bands. She discovered lyrics that encouraged drug abuse and suicide. Some lyrics were about sex and violence.

Tipper decided to do something about these lyrics. With several friends, she founded the Parents' Music Resource Center (PMRC). The women held their first meeting in May 1985. To their surprise, 350 people showed up. These people were angry at the music industry. They felt that record companies were not taking responsibility for the products they sold.

Tipper Gore feels a strong devotion to her family. Here she is pictured with three of her children as well as the Clinton family.

The National Parent Teacher Association (PTA) decided to help Tipper. The PTA donated money and told its members about the PMRC. Tipper also got help from a man inside the music industry. He helped Tipper find the right people to talk to. He explained to her how the music industry works. This man asked Tipper to never tell anyone his name. He was afraid of losing his job.

Tipper began talking to leaders in the music industry. She asked them to put a label on albums with explicit lyrics. Explicit lyrics are ones that talk about drugs, sex, violence, or suicide.

Rock musicians found out about the PMRC. Some of them were angry. They thought Tipper was trying to suppress their music or tell them what kind of music to play. This is called censorship. But Tipper made it clear that she was against censorship. She wanted record companies to voluntarily let parents and teenagers know which albums had explicit lyrics.

Before long, people all over the country were talking about explicit song lyrics. Newspapers and magazines ran articles on the subject. Leaders of the PMRC were interviewed on almost a hundred television shows. Then, in September 1985, Senator John Danforth of Missouri asked the U.S. Senate to hold a hearing about the issue.

The hearing worried Tipper. She was afraid that the senators would try to pass a law. She was against censorship laws. The hearing was held on September 19. It was one of the most watched Senate hearings in history. After the hearing, the PMRC and the record industry came to an agreement. The people who make records would voluntarily put warning labels on albums with explicit lyrics. But there would be no laws against them. The labels would say "Explicit Lyrics—Parental Advisory."

Tipper felt that she had won a great victory. But it had been a hard fight. People had said many cruel and untrue things about her. Rock singer Frank Zappa had called her a "cultural terrorist." He thought that she was trying to destroy the culture of the young generation. Many people agreed with him.

Tipper remained a member of the PMRC. The group continued to teach parents and teachers about explicit song lyrics. Soon, Tipper began writing a book about her fight for clean music.

RUNNING FOR PRESIDENT

In April 1987, Tipper was ready to publish her book, *Raising PG Kids in an X-Rated Society.* One evening, Al told her that he wanted to run for president of the United States. Tipper got mad. She had already sacrificed one career when her husband ran for Congress. Now, she was in the middle of the publicity tour for her book. He was asking her to give that up, too. They decided to think about it for ten days.

"It was an agonizing ten days," said Tipper. "I went back and forth." Finally, they decided that Al would run.

Al Gore did not do well in his campaign for president. He was stiff and uncomfortable with crowds. He never laughed or put people at ease. Tipper did all she could to help his campaign, as she had in 1976, but it was no use. Al was defeated.

THE ACCIDENT

Then, in 1989, the Gore family suffered a tragedy. Al and Albert III, their youngest child, were leaving a Baltimore Orioles baseball game. Suddenly, Albert darted into traffic and a car hit him. He was thrown 30 feet. His legs and ribs were broken. Several internal organs were crushed. Doctors weren't sure whether he would live.

For a month Albert lay in the hospital. Tipper and Al sat by his bedside. Finally, he was allowed to go home. His parents set up a bed for him in their dining room and took turns sleeping on a mattress nearby.

In the hospital, Albert had told his parents that he couldn't get well without them. They did everything they could to make sure his recovery was complete.

The accident was difficult for the family. Al blamed himself that it happened. Tipper admitted that she felt anger at her husband. The family saw a counselor and worked through their emotions. "I think because of the time we spent together, we've become much stronger as a family," says Tipper.

THE 1992 CAMPAIGN

When the next presidential campaign came around in 1992, Tipper and Al decided that Al would not run. Albert's accident and Al's defeat in 1988 had been hard on the family. Both parents wanted time to devote to their children. They didn't want to put their children through the grueling demands of a campaign.

In spite of these feelings, the family was excited when Governor Bill Clinton of Arkansas chose Al as his running mate. A campaign for vice-president would be much shorter than a campaign for president. It would be less of a strain on the family. They looked forward to it with enthusiasm.

Tipper once again proved a top-notch campaigner. She joked with the press. She even squirted them with a water pistol. One night her husband appeared as a guest on a television show. Tipper called the show without saying who she was and flirted with him. The audience loved it!

Tipper called the campaign "the most positive, exhilarating experience" she had ever had. She was touched by all the people who wanted to meet her. Children in wheelchairs, patients on oxygen—so many people wanted to shake her hand and wish her well. They believed she and her husband could help solve some of the nation's problems.

Tipper proved to be a top-notch campaigner during the 1992 Presidential race. Here she is with her husband, Al Gore, after his acceptance speech for V. P.

The Clintons and the Gores boarding a bus for a marathon campaign trip around America.

A STRONG FRIENDSHIP

For Tipper, one of the best things about the campaign was getting to know Hillary Rodham Clinton. Hillary, Bill Clinton's wife and political partner, became a good friend.

The two women barely knew each other before the campaign began. And they are very different from one another. Hillary is a successful lawyer. Tipper has concentrated on being a homemaker. But they liked each other immediately. Their energetic dance at the Democratic Convention was the beginning of a great friendship.

Soon after the convention, the Clintons and the Gores boarded buses for a marathon campaign trip around America. They stopped at big cities and small towns. They talked to people and won votes. During the trip, Tipper and Hillary shared many secrets. "Just imagine two couples on a bus for four or five days," explained Tipper. "It's really been very intimate."

The women found that they had much in common. They had both grown up during the 1960s. They shared the same political beliefs. Tipper called Hillary her "long-lost sister." Hillary called Tipper "a real partner, . . . somebody who sees the world as I do."

THE IMPORTANCE OF FAMILY

Tipper and Hillary also talked about their families. Hillary's daughter Chelsea was twelve years old. Tipper's children were teenagers. Both women worried about the effect the campaign would have on their children. And what if they won? They wanted to give their children normal lives, in spite of the pressures they would feel being the children of the president and vice-president.

Tipper and Al had always devoted time to their four children, in spite of their busy lives. They had made two homes for the family, one in Washington, D.C., and the other in Arlington. The family also visited Carthage, where Al's parents still live.

All the Gores are athletic. They enjoy waterskiing, swimming, hiking, and in-line skating. In 1989, Al gave Tipper a pair of Rollerblades for her fortieth birthday.

The three daughters play soccer and lacrosse at school. Kristin has been on the District of Columbia's girls' lacrosse team, and Karenna is a champion waterskier. Albert has recovered so well from his accident that he is now as active in sports as the rest of the family.

During the campaign, the Gores established "family days" that were off limits to staff people and the press. When Albert turned ten years old in October 1992, Tipper insisted that the campaign shut down so that the family could spend time together in Washington. Tipper also insists that her children not be photographed unless they want to be.

To their parents' relief, the Gore children enjoyed the campaign. Albert was especially outgoing. He shook hands with the crowds and signed autographs. In November, when Bill Clinton and Al Gore won the election, the whole family celebrated. They began looking forward to their new life in Washington.

A NEW ROLE IN POLITICS

Shortly after the inauguration, Tipper and her family moved into the vice-presidential house in Washington, D.C. The twelve-acre estate is on the grounds of the Naval Observatory. Tipper faces pressure as the wife of the vice-president. People will judge what she does, where she goes, and what she wears. Also, some people still are not happy about her fight against explicit rock lyrics. They wonder if she will take up similar causes. But pressure has been part of Tipper's life since she married Al Gore in 1970. With her family and friends like Hillary Clinton to support her, Tipper will surely be happy in her new role in American politics.

Tipper stands next to her husband as he is sworn in as vice-president of the United States.

GLOSSARY

Campaign - A connected series of activities designed to bring about a particular result.

Capitol - A building in which a state legislative body meets.

Civil Rights - The nonpolitical rights of a citizen.

Congress - The supreme legislative body of a nation.

Democrats - One who practices social equality.

Democratic National Convention - Gathering of the Democratic party for the purpose of selecting a presidential candidate.

The draft - A method for selecting individuals for a group.

Explicit - Fully revealed or expressed plan.

Inauguration - A ceremonial induction into office.

Nomination - To propose as a canidate for election to office.

PMRC - Parents' Music Resource Center.

Politics - The art or science of government.

PTA - Parent Teacher Association.

Senate - A governing or lawmaking assembly.

Senator - A member of a senate.

REFERENCES

Chua-Eoan, Howard G., "First Friends." People, Nov. 16, 1992.

DeCurtis, Anthony. "Tipper: Dems Send Wrong Message." Rolling Stone, Sep. 3, 1992.

Duffy, Thom. "Wife's Crusade Has Music Biz Wary of Gore." Billboard, July 25, 1992.

Gail Sheehy. Character: America's Search for Leadership. (New York: Morrow, 1988)

Gleick, Elizabeth, and Margie Sellinger. "Tipper's Return." People, July 27, 1992.

Gore, Tipper. Raising PG Kids in an X-Rated Society. (Nashville, Tenn.: Abingdon, 1987).

Lacayo, Richard. "Tipper: The Other Partner." Time, July 20, 1992.

Miller, Judith. "The Cooki-Cutter Wives of Politics." Vogue, Nov. 1992.

O'Neill, Molly. "Striking a Political Note, Stumbling on a Pronoun." New York Times, Oct. 27, 1992.

INDEX

Aitcheson, John - 6
Aitcheson, Mary Elizabeth - 6
Campaign - 15, 20, 22, 25-27
Civil Rights - 9
Clinton, Bill - 4, 25, 27
Clinton, Chelsea - 26
Clinton, Hillary Rodham - 4, 25, 26, 28
Congress - 15, 20
Danforth, Senator John - 18
Democratic National Convention - 4, 25
The draft - 11
Gore, Albert, Sr. - 7, 11
Gore, Albert III - 16, 27
Gore, Karenna - 15, 16, 27
Gore, Kristin - 16
Gore, Nancy - 9, 15
Gore, Pauline - 7
Gore, Sarah - 16
Harvard University - 9
Naval Observatory - 28
Parents' Music Resource Center - 16, 18-20, 28
Parent Teacher Association - 18, 19
Senator - 7, 11, 15, 18, 19
Vanderbilt Law School - 7
Vietnam - 9, 11
Zappa, Frank - 19